LENA CLOVIS

MANAGE STRESS

**The Ultimate Guide on Stress Management, Learn the
Secrets and Best Strategies on How You Can Overcome
Stress and Avoid Stress Buildup**

Descrierea CIP a Bibliotecii Naţionale a României
LENA CLOVIS
    MANAGE   STRESS.   The   Ultimate   Guide   on   Stress
Management, Learn the Secrets and Best Strategies on How
You Can Overcome Stress and Avoid Stress Buildup /Lena
Clovis – Bucharest: Editura My Ebook, 2021
    ISBN

LENA CLOVIS

MANAGE STRESS

The Ultimate Guide on Stress Management, Learn the Secrets and Best Strategies on How You Can Overcome Stress and Avoid Stress Buildup

My Ebook Publishing House
Bucharest, 2021

TABLE OF CONTENTS

INTRODUCTION

Nobody likes having to deal with stress on a daily basis. Most of the time, anyone with an ounce of sanity left in their body will always choose to avoid any stressful situations at any cost, which is why we've decided to come up with this book for you.

Stress tends to be the crutch of humanity. While most other creatures out there would most likely use stress to their advantage in order to pull through any serious life threatening situations, we tend to take a different approach when it comes to facing off against stressful situations. We usually either freeze up, leaving us completely vulnerable against any danger whatsoever, or we end up running away with our tails between our legs.

This is the sad truth behind humanity as a whole, we don't usually know how to deal with stress or what even causes it in the first place. For example, did you know that stress used to be like a sort of spider sense for us, allowing us to foresee dangerous situations approaching us, telling us that we need to either fight it out or flee with our lives? Yes, that's right, we used to be dependent on feelings such as stress and fear, since they would force us to pull through inhumane conditions and increase the chances of our survival as a species. Regardless of the past though, we no longer require stress as a tool in order to fight it out for our survival.

Nowadays we are taught that our survivability is already conferred to us, and instead we should concentrate on our passions and hobbies. Although this sounds good at first, this has caused us to become fragile, unwilling to be able to deal with emotions such as stress and fear.

So, despite the fact that stress is meant to help us pull through hard to deal with situations, nowadays stress seems to be nothing more than a bothersome anchor that's holding us down. Sure, there are plenty of people that can still use stress to their advantage, but alas, too much stress can break anyone, regardless of how powerful they may be mentally or physically.

In here we will be discussing and presenting you with all of the information that you need in order to manage your stress levels better. This book includes answers to questions such as
8

"What is stress?" and "How can we avoid stress inducing situations?" while also providing you with activities that you can occupy your free time with in order to avoid stress build-up. So, without further ado, let's answer the first question that we get asked most of the time, aka "What is stress in the first place?"

CHAPTER 1

STRESS: THE GOOD, THE BAD

AND THE UGLY

When you think about stress you most likely think about it in a negative way, don't you? Well we're here to tell you that stress is not always a bad thing. First and foremost, stress is a feeling that we get when things are getting a bit too intense for our own liking. This most likely means that you're in over your head and that you're not able to process everything that you have on your plate at the moment. For example, if you have to deal with multiple projects at the same time and you find out that your partner is no longer able to commit himself/herself to the job anymore. That feeling of helplessness and complete exposure to the mental/physical attack is unbelievably hard to deal with. But that's not what the emotion was made for originally.

Back in the old days of Neanderthal humans, stress was a sort of a "Spider sense" that would work in our favor in order to make sure that we knew that we were in over our heads and that our lives were at stake at that point. As a result, most of us were literally forced by our bodies to choose one of three options: Fight, Flee or Freeze. Couple this with the fact that our bodies would start pumping out adrenaline and you have one ferocious beast with one single purpose in life: Survive. But alas, we are no longer Neanderthals, quite the contrary actually. Stress has gained quite a negative connotation because it literally only does one thing anymore: Make things harder for us.

Yes, that's right, stress has started as one of our survival kit's most valuable tools, and yet it became one of our most deadly handicaps. Most of us are no longer as fearless as we used to be, quite the contrary actually. We are but shadows of our past versions which would fight for the right to survive on a daily basis. Since our lives are so disconnected from the wildlife we tend to choose one of the other two options most of the time, aka: Flee or Freeze. If we're lucky enough to manage to choose the first option then we'll most likely get out with our pride unscathed, but the problem is that most of the time we can't help but freeze in place and stand there, ready to absorb any damage we get.

But stress is a lot more than that. Some people, albeit a more remote number of people, tend to be able to use stress to their advantage and progress as a result to that special skill. Instead of fleeing or freezing, they take it as a challenge and end up improving as a result. Although this doesn't work for everyone, there are still plenty of people that can be added to this category.

But anyways, that's the history of stress as a whole. It can be good, it can be bad, and it can sure as hell be ugly, but if we can use it to our advantage we can definitely improve as a whole. So, without delving even farther into the rabbit hole, let's concentrate on another important aspect regarding stress, aka how to avoid it in the first place.

CHAPTER 2

AVOIDING THE UNAVOIDABLE

Yes, most of the time stress is unavoidable, but the thing is that we never actually try to prevent it which leads to way more stress as a result to our poor planning. So, the truth is that even though sometimes stress build-up is unstoppable, we can work our way through avoiding most of it and diminishing the impact of the unavoidable one. Yep, it sounds a bit confusing, so let's explain this better with the following examples:

- **Live a more active life**

Let's be honest here, the more stressful people are the less active they are in their spare time. This is why we need to work on maintaining that sweaty lifestyle until we have no reason to actually complain anymore. Exercising can be its own reward but let's be honest here, the more active we are, the less time we spend over thinking things. Now, we don't mean that you should go the steroid route, quite the contrary actually. We just mean a jog every morning coupled with maybe going to the gym every 2 days or so while also drinking lots of water and maybe even picking up a dancing class or such. Whatever makes you happy is going to be worth it in the end, don't forget that.

- **Eat Healthier**

You know the saying "Can't think straight without a good meal?" Well, this is 100% the truth since the less healthy we are when it comes to our nutrition the more likely we are to be stressed out of our minds. This is why maintaining a healthy lifestyle is such a good idea for your mind and body.

You can even try to go for a vegan/vegetarian lifestyle, but don't consider it a requirement.

Whatever you eat, make sure that it's healthy enough to keep your body energized and happy throughout the day.

Vegan/vegetarian options are always a good choice to make, even if you don't necessarily plan on going down that route. A vegan burger is better than no burger, although nobody will complain if you treat yourself with a sandwich every now and then, as long as it's not fast food.

- **Socialize more**

The more time you spend with your friends and family, the more relaxed you'll be which is why this is so important. Call your parents and tell them that you love them, if you have a significant other then make sure that you take them out tonight, buy them flowers, even if you're not usually the one giving out the presents. Keep your friends close and your family even closer and you'll be living out your days stress- free, unless of course family has some ties to your stress, in which case it's best to concentrate on your friends and significant other.

- **Compliment yourself**

Yep, this is a weird one, but we can't argue with the results. As long as you let yourself know that you're doing okay, that you look your best and that you don't need to put yourself down anymore you should be able to avoid stress most of the time. So, for this exercise, go to the closest mirror you can find and look at yourself in the mirror. Instead of picking everything apart, how about complimenting yourself for once?

Is your hair looking better today than it usually does?

Whatever you can find, say it to yourself. You would be shocked to find out how many people tend to ignore their positives and instead concentrate on the negative parts in their lives. Don't let yourself become a victim to your own self-consciousness issues. Fight through by complimenting yourself on a daily basis.

CHAPTER 3

MEDITATION OVER MEDICATION

Pills can do a lot of good things, but they should never be used to deal with stress problems. This is because stress should not be considered a disease. We need to consider it as it is: A signal pointing out that we're in over our heads. This basically means that we need to use mind numbing techniques such as meditation in order to pull through any stressful situation.

Yoga helps a lot; just spend your time concentrating on your form and such instead of working on things that you can't do anything about. Meditate for a good hour and a half a day and we can assure you that your mind will be way clearer than before which will cause your stress levels to lower almost instantaneously.

This might be hard to do at first, but it'll be worth it on the long run. Unless you're a psychopath that's devoid of all emotions you should be able to maintain a positive mindset on a daily basis.

Sure, it might sound a bit fake at first, but that doesn't really matter when the fact is that you will most likely improve your mental state this way over a relatively short period of time.

This is a sort of a "fake it until you make it" type of an ordeal, but if you do remind yourself to keep a positive mindset at all times then you should be able to avoid any stress build-up over the course of the day. In order to help you maintain that happiness level up and that stress level down you can also use media to your advantage. Turn off that depressing news station and instead how about you turn to some childish cartoons? Listen to happy-go- lucky music for once, try some Swing music from the 50s and relax. Life is good; there is no reason to pollute your mind with negativity and stress.

CHAPTER 4

HELP THOSE AROUND YOU

Your mental state is usually affected by what you see around you. If you see some homeless people begging at the side of the road and then you hear that your girlfriend/boyfriend has had to deal with a lot of stress that day then you'll most likely become quite stressed as a result of that too. In order to avoid this from happening you need to make sure that you help those around you. The more people you help improve their lifestyles the better since you'll also feel better as a result of that.

So, why not call your mother or father? Ask them how they are, tell them that you love them, that you miss them, tell them that you should hang out more, buy them flowers or whatever might make them happy, etc. Whatever it is, just remember to always respect those around you since mistreating those around you will cause you to look back more, which will in turn make you more stressed.

CHAPTER 5

IMPROVE DON'T DISAPPROVE

Instead of complaining about how you look or how you act, you need to make sure that you're always improving yourself with every mistake. Sure, that mistake you made probably cost you a lot more than you wanted it to, but alas, as long as you learn from it and make sure that it never happens again that is no longer categorized as a mistake anymore. It is a stone that you can use to propel yourself even higher, becoming a better version of yourself as a whole.

Stop disapproving yourself and comparing yourself to everyone around you. You have your positives and they have theirs, you have your high points and so do they, and at the end of the day we all know what being overstressed feels like and not one of us likes it. So, instead of overreacting to every issue you come across, how about you analyze it carefully and move forward with a new strategy in order to avoid those circumstances from ever repeating in the first place.

CHAPTER 6

TREAT YOURSELF THE WAY
YOU WANT TO BE TREATED

When's the last time that you decided that you needed a break? When's the last time that you treated yourself to some alone time, in which you enjoy your own company and treat yourself to whatever you want to get? If you're dealing with a lot of stress then the answer to that is probably "not for a long time now".

That's one of the reasons as to why we are so stressed most of the time. We all need a break every now and then, and that's a fact. We are not robots, we can't work for months and months and only see to it that those around us have everything that they need to enjoy themselves. We deserve our breaks just as much as everyone else does, which is why this is so important for our mental states.

So, how about you take a much needed vacation somewhere this weekend? If you have the budget for it then you can always go for the classic "throw dart at a world map and see where it hits", but if you prefer something more casual how about you instead just go to a local forest and enjoy nature for a bit? Pick up a book, take your dog out for a walk, go jogging, go to the local park and eat an ice cream in the blazing sun. You choose whatever makes you happy, regardless of how costly it may or may not be. You're doing this for yourself, remember that. You're not doing this for Jim from management, you're not doing this for your snobby sibling or you're obnoxious boss. You're the target of this experiment and you earned this, so you might as well enjoy it.

CHAPTER 7

AVOID CAFFEINE, ALCOHOL,

AND NICOTINE

This shouldn't shock anyone, but being exposed to these "special ingredients" is never a good idea. Sure, alcohol never hurts if you're being careful with how much you consume on a daily basis, it can even be healthy if you know how to regulate your drinking, but if you're already dealing with stress then a bottle of alcohol is never a good idea. Take it this way: keep alcohol as a reward, not as a ledge to hold onto in a difficult time, because that ledge will soon turn into a skippering slope and before you know it you'll be falling down the pit of despair harder than ever before.

Same goes for caffeine and nicotine. People tend to believe that caffeine does nothing bad to you since it had the ability to help you actually keep your eyes open, but at the end of the day if you rely too much on that morning coffee then you'll soon realize the fact that you cannot function properly without having siphoned at least a couple of cups per day. Not only that, but this can also damage your teeth which will lead to even more stress.

Nicotine wise, you already know the whole ordeal. Smoking is not healthy, and even though it can be relaxing to most it should never be used as a crutch to help get past stressful situations.

Sleep is important, we all know that, and although we might not always have a choice about when we wake up or go to sleep, it should always come as a priority to get at least 6 hours of sleep every night. 8 hours of sleep is the best way to deal with stress, but let's be honest here, most of the time we don't really get a choice regarding this. So, just try your hardest to keep your eyes shut for at least 6 hours straight and you'll see a difference in no time.

CHAPTER 8

GET A DIARY AND START WRITING

This is an important one as it helps you deal with your surroundings in a non-aggressive way. Write down your deepest desires, your biggest fears, your accomplishments and embarrassing moments. Whatever comes to your mind, just write it all down and you'll immediately see a difference in your mental state. You can even try to write down letters to everyone that has angered you this week and such and burn them after you're done writing them.

Warning: Never actually send the letters. This isn't the plot of neither a romance movie nor a comedy. This is your life and you should treat it as such. Actually, sending them will lead to even more stressful situations and before you know it, you'll be dealing with plenty more stress than before. It's best to just bottle it up then throw all of your emotions into that diary.

CHAPTER 9

USE YOUR FREE TIME CAREFULLY

And the more stress-free you are during the day the more likely you are to avoid escalating any argument with anyone.

Eating healthier is always a must if you want to avoid having any health problems, but it can also help you with stress reduction.

This will also help you become a better version Start exercising, follow your hobbies, do whatever makes you happy. Do whatever you can so you can end the day knowing that you've accomplished something. Although this might sound a bit cheesy, maintaining a healthy lifestyle is always a good way to waste your time because it increases your self-confidence while also giving you a way to relieve yourself of all of that stress.

Most of the time the people that spend their days in the gym tend to waste all of that extra energy in there, leaving them stress-free for the rest of the day. It's a great way to relieve all of that stress of yourself which will lead to an increased self-confidence which in return makes you better at dealing with stressful situations. It's all pretty simple, really. You just need to realize the fact that the more you work on improving yourself the better you'll be at dealing with uncomfortable situations. The more you deal with these types of issues the more likely you are to become better at deescalating them before they become detrimental to your own sanity.

Meditation will always hope a stressful mind and body because it helps you focus on what is really important in life. Mindfulness will help you increase your mental range and help you develop a new perspective on life as a whole. The more you practice this mental muscle the easier it will become to keep your mind intact when a stressful situation arises. You can release all of your negative emotions right then and there and not have to throw them around coupled with accusations which lead to even more stress.

This is one of the few steps that actually provides immediate benefits if done correctly. If you fully commit yourself to this practice then you will definitely see changes in less than a month's time. Just remember to keep a positive mindset on life and you'll be good to go most of the time.

CHAPTER 10

FIND A PURPOSE AND WORK ON IT

This is a difficult step since it all depends on the person at hand. If you're good at dealing with this sort of stuff and already know what to work on then this will come as second nature to you, but just in case, let's explain this a bit more thoroughly. You need to find something that's both achievable and entertaining for you to chase after. The reason behind this is the fact that you want to have to work for this, but you don't want it to become another stress causing issue. You want it to be a game, but at the same time you need it to occupy just enough mental processing that it causes you to stop worrying about those around you and such.

Alternatively, you can also pick up a new hobby, like painting or soccer or such. Whatever it is, as long as it keeps you entertained and stress-free it's worth every second spend on it.

CHAPTER 11

ACCEPT YOURSELF FOR WHO YOU ARE;
IMPERFECTIONS AND ALL

Most of the time the reason as to why we are so stressed is because we have certain expectations that we need to reach otherwise we allow our stress to eat us up from the inside. In order to avoid this, you need to stop worrying about being the best and instead accept yourself the way you are. Stop striving for greatness and instead commend yourself for being able to get this far in the first place.

It's definitely going to be hard at first, but the process will be worth it. Stress can cause a ton of problems, including serious physical issues that we need to face later on in life as a result to our carelessness. Don't allow these to bottle up, fix them before it's too late.

CHAPTER 12

"SLEEP IS MORE IMPORTANT THAN FOOD"

This might sound a bit weird at first, but it is the truth. Six hours per night is more important than three meals a day because without sleep you cannot even think straight anymore. Sure, thinking on an empty stomach is hard too, but if you get less than six hours of sleep then you legit won't be able to think about anything but falling into a coma every 2-3 seconds.

This is why you need to strive for the golden eight hours of sleep every night, or at least go for a good six hours to make sure that your mind's rested and ready for action. You cannot, and I repeat, cannot absolutely under no circumstances mess up your sleep pattern. If you frequently go to sleep at 4-5 AM and you need to wake up at 8 then you need to change that up right away because that is in no way shape or form a good way to deal with stress.

Before you know it you'll be a walking zombie ready to play in the latest season of AMC's The Walking Dead.

CHAPTER 13

"KEEP AN ACTIVE LIFESTYLE"

Being active has always been a good way to maintain a positive outlook on life. It is a known fact that the more active you are the happier you get because you no longer spend your time worrying about anything non-consequential to your life anymore. You focus on what's in front of you, on what really matters, which ends up being a really good way of avoiding stress as a whole. So, if you want to make sure that you're stress free most of the time all that you need is to keep that blood pumping and that adrenaline up.

Do morning jogging sessions, go to the gym, and enjoy a cold bottle of water after exercising for a good hour or so. Every little bit helps, and that's a fact.

Most people that have to deal with stress overload tend to feel empty every time they have any spare time on their hands. This is because they cannot concentrate on anything but the work that they've been handling for the past couple of days.

So, instead of soaking in all of this how about you instead focus on a brand new hobby, aka something to help you release stress while also preventing future stress from piling up on your psyche?

It's a great exercise to work on and a really useful way of get your mind off of things that you do not wish to concentrate on at the moment. Try a new sport, maybe pick up some dancing classes, whatever helps you sleep better at night knowing you did something better with your time than just gloat over what you didn't do right lately.

CHAPTER 14

"FORGET ABOUT YOURSELF;

CONCENTRATE ON THOSE AROUND YOU INSTEAD"

As mentioned previously, we tend to focus too much on our problems, to the point where they become detrimental to our own minds and bodies. This is why instead of focusing on our own problems; a good way to handle stress buildup is to literally just change your perspective altogether and look for a new horizon to brighten up. So, in simpler terms, help those around you more.

Buy your mother a bouquet of flowers; buy your dad a much earned shaving set, whatever makes them happier at the end of the day.

Luckily though, most of the time when it comes to giving presents to your friends and family members the thought is all that matters.

So, as long as you do actually buy them something it shouldn't be that hard to choose what you do actually want to give them.

Again, it's the thought that matters, and we can assure you that you'll be gaining just as much as they do, if not more.

CHAPTER 15

"AVOID ANY AND ALL ADDICTIVE SUBSTANCES"

Now, of course that we're not referring to crack cocaine here or anything like that. What we mean is that you should probably take a while off addictive substances such as nicotine, caffeine and alcohol until you get your mind straight. It will be tough at first, especially if you're neck deep in your addiction, but we can assure you that those things are only worsening your current situation.

There is no need for them in your life, no need whatsoever, so how about you give them a good old push and just like that try living your life on the safer side of the spectrum? It's not a requirement that you give up on them as a whole either. All that you need to do is you need to make sure that you're limiting their use and just like that you've already made progress.

CHAPTER 16

"LAUGH IT OUT"

Maintaining a positive outlook on your life as a whole is very good for yourself because it helps you cope with everything bad that's happening to you. Most of the time we tend to bottle everything up until we can't help but explode, causing a ruckus for both us and everyone around us. In order to avoid this from happening you need to keep that positive attitude up at all times. Use whatever means you can in order to preserve that smile too, such as happy-go-lucky music and comedy films. Whatever helps you pull through without overworking yourself and your inner psyche will eventually help you prevent any upcoming stress overloads.

CHAPTER 17

"STOP PROCRASTINATING"

This is a big one, and one of the most important parts in the process of avoiding stress buildup because it deals with one of the main causes of stress buildup. Procrastination is a terrible sin that we're all guilty in taking a part in regardless of whether we want to or not. So, in order to make sure that we don't end up exploding randomly one day we need to make sure that we don't procrastinate anymore.

This is, again, very important because it is both easier and harder than any other step in this list. It all depends on how powerful your will is. If your will is strong enough you should have no problem with getting past this hurdle, and once you do you'll immediately start seeing a difference.

9 786069 837634

Printed by Libri Plureos GmbH in Hamburg, Germany